Heaven & Earth Holding Company

PITT POETRY SERIES   Ed Ochester, Editor

Heaven & Earth Holding Company

JOHN HODGEN

University of Pittsburgh Press

Published by the University of Pittsburgh Press,

Pittsburgh, Pa., 15260

Manufactured in the United States of America

Printed on acid-free paper

10   9   8   7   6   5   4   3   2   1

ISBN 13: 978-0-8229-6114-7

ISBN 10: 0-8229-6114-8

For my family, my friends, and for love . . .
what else?

✳

i carry your heart (i carry it in my heart)
e e cummings

CONTENTS

II . . . crawling between . . .

III . . . in your philosophy. . .

I   . . . must i remember? . . .

Undiscovering America

Somewhere today, on some ethereal preserve, all the old explorers
gather in Manhattan for one of those trendy group photo shoots,
some meet-and-greet publicity tour for the History Channel.
They clank onto a loading dock with their breastplates and swords,
navigating among each other, bumptious, grumpy
in their puffy pantaloons, their helmets curved like half-moons.
They shake hands all around, gruffly, line up roughly alphabetically:
Balboa pressing forward, Cabot saying cheese, Columbus, of course,
Coronado, Cortez, dodgy DeSoto, Vasco da Gama and old Ponce de Leon,
nervous Magellan in his Arrow shirt, black-hatted Father Marquette, his cellmate, Joliet,
coon-skinned Zebulon Pike peeking out, Pocahontas holding hands with John Smith,
Sacajawea, smiling, like the Land O'Lakes maiden, between Lewis and Clark,
and lonely Vespucci at the end of the row, mumbling to himself
his mother's regrets, *Amerigo, Amerigo.*

After the shoot is over, Francisco Pizarro, the group spokesperson,
announces that they are leaving America, all of them, going back, going home,
sailing backward down the Hudson for the Southeast Passage,
in their tall ships, the Golden Hind, Nina, Pinta, Santa Maria,
past the Port Authority, the Statue of Liberty, past the Hamptons,
past the Fountain of Youth, the Seven Lost Cities of Gold,
past the Pathfinders and Explorers backed up on their way to the mall,
till their ships look like toy boats, toy boats, till their ships are so small,
till they sit at the edge of the world, till they fall,
saying this is not what we were looking for, this is not it at all.

Girl with Her Tongue Stuck Out

Made to stand for hours in the center of the living room,
sticking the small red plum of her tongue out, *out*,
to prove to her father that the cat hadn't gotten it,

knowing even then that she would repeat third grade,
would dummy up to the dust that collected in the corner,
would play right field, the others yelling *swing, batter, batter,*

would button her lip, misspell "dumbbell" in the spelling bee,
would never give anyone the raspberry, ever, *ever,*
not even Michael "Icky" Snay, knowing even then

that Speak-No-Evil was the monkey on her back,
that the best child, the best child, was seen, only seen,
and that someday she would speak in the whispers of the trees,

but not today, not just yet, not this minute,
not with him hissing in his chair, seething, seething,
the red cat perched straight up on his lap, licking its chops.

Just a Tranquil Darker

The old woman asks if she can have her sunglasses *just a tranquil darker*,
and the optometrist, without blinking an eye, says he can do that, he'll take care
of that for her. And I think for a moment that he is William Wordsworth listening
to Dorothy, her spontaneous overflow of powerful feelings, her perfect tranquility.
Or maybe he is God himself, the great optometrist, or at least that dim image we strain
to see of the omniscient optician who mostly does not trifle with us. The occasional hat
flown off our heads, perhaps, the tossed banana peel with the businessman's wingtip
approaching, the hurtling safe heading down toward our heads, all of us so intensely looking
elsewhere, as if our lives were God's *New Yorker* cartoons, all his back issues stacked up,
the ones with the Elizabeth Bishop poems, teetering, in his waiting room.

Mostly He gives us our due, God, or Wordsworth for that matter, for the things we choose
to believe in, the things we say we'll see if we can do, like loving each other, like being true,
like the woman who accompanies her husband, the lawn-mowing man, and sits on the steps
of the houses he goes to. (See her, by the daffodils?) She watches him moving from row
to row, loves the ease with which he moves, sees the lawn changing right before her eyes,
like some eye chart of I's and E's slowly coming into view, her love for him the one thing
that is perfectly clear. It is as if they live in some peripheral light that is always glowing,
that we can see sometimes, like a lark that flares up suddenly out of the corner of our eyes,
somehow always lifting from this cockeyed part of the world, away from the glare,
to some other place where everything is just the way we want it, just a tranquil darker.

When Dylan Left Hibbing, Minnesota, August 1959

Not even Dylan then, more like David the Blue-Eyed Shepherd Boy Giant Killer instead,

the way he must have looked in those *Golden Book Illustrated Bible Stories* we never read,

the ones with the pictures of the prophets, each with a gold record stuck to his head,

or the Classic Comics *Crime and Punishment*, Raskolnikov rocking and rolling on his bed,

heading on down the highway out of St. Petersburg, the landlord's axe still in the shed,

throwing stones at all the stop signs a-bleeding in his head.

Wasn't he a singing terrorist then, slaying us in the aisles, knocking us dead,

like some wild-eyed kid from Fallujah now, his machine gun guitar slipped over his head,

his ass in a sling, his mind full of dynamite, his righteous streets turning red,

his only song his heaven's door, toward which he runs, arms outspread.

Oh, Zimmerman, we never heard a single word you ever said,

from Ararats to ziggurats, from alpha down to zed,

our heads cut off, our tongues cut out, no words left to be said,

all the things we've ever loved, dead, dead, dead, dead.

High Tide

A man I know named Watters commanded riverboats during the war in Vietnam. He drilled

through the heart of the Mekong. Now he teaches peace studies to wide-eyed kids,

the arc of his life having turned him this way, utterly, as if by design. They stare at him,

silent as fish. He says he is casting his nets. He says power corrupts, peace through strength.

He says MIRV, SEATO, NATO, MAD. He says new submarines, launching platforms,

multiple warhead killing machines, Ohio Class (Ohio so centered, so far from the sea,

except in the Ice Age, the glacial moraine), the new Ohios under icecaps again, circling

the world smoothly, almost silently. He says there are things he cannot say. He says *expiate*.

His eyes fill up. He turns away. And this man with whom I am comfortable kayaks

in the summer all over the world, in Alaska, the Aleutians, where Inuits since the Ice Age

have hunted whales the size of submarines. And he has married a woman from Ohio,

whom he loves smoothly, almost silently, more than he can say, even loving her name, Edith,

a name that doesn't sit well among popular women's names, a name she herself doesn't like,

but one that he loves just because it is her name. I tell him he is the only man I know who can

have his kayak and Edith too. Like a fish out of water, I tell him, like Onitsura's haiku.

He smiles, says sometimes he flips his kayak deliberately over and over in the Bay of Fundy,

turning the fragmented world on its axis again and again, smoothly, almost silently,

world into water, water into shimmering light.

Romance

You say words diminish the thing that is said,

and you hold your truth tightly, those words, at least, undiminished,

resounding, like a ten-penny nail driven home, driven dead.

But each word has its worth, its intimations, each tremulous hem and haw wished

into being like baby wrens, all beaks, squawks, then shoved into the coarse air, pushed,

hard-loved, from their nests, into nothing but hopes of wobbly, Kitty Hawked flight.

Some drop straight away, as if skeet shot, heart-stoned, not even flapping, dashed

dizzy, bird-brained on the rocks, the cold ridges. Some are done in, undone by the tight

metaphysics of the world, its limitations, its negative capabilities. And some are hushed

into a silence almost palpable, their secret hearts made of nothing so much as pure dread.

Believe this. In World War II, bent-winged fighter planes, Corsairs, whooshed

off aircraft carrier flight decks, then dropped partially, momentarily, completely from sight,

the pilots saying their own words perhaps, *Lord*, or *Mother*, or *Oh shit, I'm dead*,

but then they lifted, miraculously, climbed, swooped, whooped, barrel-rolled in the air,

no rhyme, little reason, hearts in their throats, a wordless word, an undiminished prayer.

Keats

Plane back from Portland, Motion's *Keats* on my lap, bright sun on the wing,

like a perfect bowl, its own little sun, the light like the world holding on, holding on.

Light that we reach for, even right at the end, while we cling to our pain, this swath on the wing,

so intense, so seeming substantial, that I long to be in it, to be it, the way it struggles, hangs on,

like the man on the wing in the old *Twilight Zone*, holding on like a madman, teeth to the wind,

his hair blown back like knives. Or the man who climbed Mt. St. Helens last week, the way

he must have felt at the top, stepping back for his picture, the snow giving way, snow bright

with the sun, wind-driven, all air, snow not to be trusted. "False promise," Keats would say,

La Belle Dame sans Merci, the man clutching at sunlight, at the air within air, hands outspread,

falling fifteen hundred feet into the bowl of the mountain, filled with that selfsame light.

Or the old woman yesterday falling down the steps, the light that flared in her eyes, that dread,

both surprised and not surprised, this coming to Jesus, spotlight upon her now, slow motion,

kinetic, wooden doll on a string, Nude Descending a Staircase, legs all akilter, hither and yon.

It has come to this, she is saying, *so this is the place I've been coming to all along.*

And Keats and Fanny Brawne, his love for her like sunlight on a nightingale's wing,

like the moonlight that gathered on the hardwood floor in the room where he lay dying

by the Spanish Steps in Rome, the light like a leaf flown in the window, gently glowing,

like a heart, so rich, so filled with palpable light that only Keats could understand,

that he could offer it to her, the light of his life, that he could hold his own heart in his hand.

**Upon Reading in Elmore Leonard's *The Hot Kid* that Church Pews
in the 1930s Were Made by Convicts**

License plates, I always thought, in the metal shop in convict hell,
in some crooked warden's Big House slammer iron-bar hotel
filled with Cagneys, Bogeys, Edward G.'s, where weasely stoolies
got the shiv, where you bribed the screws with Lucky Strikes, Pall Malls,
where Rocky Sullivan on his way to the chair ran pell-mell, cried like a drooly
girl because Pat O'Brien, the last good priest, had asked him to, to do it so well
that the Dead End Kids would think he was yellow, had pissed himself,
so they'd go back to their homework, grow up to be priests themselves.

License plates, Georgia's sweet Peach, Pennsylvania's Keystone,
Wyoming's rider on a bucking bronc, North Dakota's Peace Garden,
bright Florida's Sunshine, lonely New Hampshire's Live Free or Die,
and somewhere in Sing Sing, Rikers, or Attica, Montana's big Big Sky.
All those dreams, that license, all those places to go. Not pews though,
Judas Priest, not stinking Jonathan Edwards Jesus pews, row after row,
on which to squirm, where children would sit, convicted already, ashamed,
angels with dirty faces, their little legs dangling like spiders over the flames.

Killing Mice, December

Four this month alone, three more than the norm per annum in previous years, some nest,
infestation, some chance, however slim, of one getting into the house, my animus rising,
cool, dispassionate, like a tiny temperate storm. And I do not use the Hav-a-Heart, no tech
support, I who routinely open windows, doors, to help a fly get back outside, before it turns
to husk and dust, to find its airy home again. Lord knows I do not have a heart, the wooden
slat enough for me, the tiny Gericault Medusa raft, the pallet with the spring-action, built-in
metal bar that cracks their backs, their heads, their hearts, so quickly, effectually, dead in
their droppings, their tracks, except the once, the trap dragged clear across the cool shed floor,
that life shed more slowly, there, while I was gone, the heart beating clearly. I do not care.
I would if the body moved, of course, when I went to pick up the trap, my hand arched widely
over it, like some little rainbow, some lavish god, the mousetail drooping, Poe's pendulum,
spent, as I dangle it, without touching it, over the black Glad bag, drop it inside with a plop.
I have read *The Plague*, know my rats, ersatz, my mycenaeum, know Hamlet's *Mousetrap*,
prologue-less, his knavish piece of work. I know my Mickey, Minnie, Mouseketeers,
my beastie Bobby Burns, my Piper Pied, my moles, voles, my knee-jerk, Wolf Trap–
going, sleeve-a-heart friends, who dutifully carry their living mice, boxed, amazed,
Plato-caved, out to the woods, the airy light, release them, to have them come back in again,
visitors, inquisitors, Whack-a-mole. I tell them all to shut their traps. We're all in traps,
or heading into one, like B-movie cowboys named Dusty or Slim, or *Midnight Cowboy*'s
Ratzo Rizzo walking through traffic, sticking our necks out, our hair pulled back, slick.
We're all going to die. Just make it quick.

Sorrow

What else to do with sorrow but to buy her a drink, walk it over to her table, set it down
in front of her (Sorrow is a woman, always has been, always will), and say the only pick-up
line you've ever heard that works, *Drink this until I start to look handsome.*
She'll look down at the drink, then up at you slowly, then down at the drink again,
and say, in a voice that will make you feel that it's all right to keep drowning,
"It's going to take more than that." So you tell her you have an extra ticket to the game,
and you know already that it's going to be a good one, a long fly ball in the bottom
of the ninth, and, surprisingly, she comes, and she knows her game too, saying of the runner
stealing second, that he has a mad case of the quicks. And you realize for the first time,
and with the finality that could be the basis for starting a religion, that sorrow
is smarter than you are (always has been, always will be), and the best you can come back
with is from basketball, that men who can dunk have mad ups. And still she comes
home with you, stays for the night, standing barefoot on your lawn with you at 4:30 a.m.,
drinks in your hands, naming the stars, waiting for the birds to wake up so she can name
them all too. And you know she's moving in with you, that she'll want all new curtains,
that you'll be known as Mr. Sorrow now, that you're starting to look handsome,
that you've got a mad case of the slows, that she's yours now forever,
always has been, always will be.

Watson

"Watson, come here. I want you," Bell said, and Watson came running like a boy. What son
wouldn't come to a father like that, ringing with delight, his acid tongue turning into sound?
And Sherlock's boy Watson came running as well, dim bulb, sure thing, everything
elementary except to him, the watts on his fixture lower than the norm. He took joy at being
called, simple as that, the sea of questions, demands, each one hounding him, swirling
like a thousand Copley sharks. It didn't even matter what it was that he was called for.
As if Holmes, all his *whats* and *whys*, his withering condescension, which was uncalled for,
was where the heart was. As if Watson were some winsome college boy from Whatsamatta
U., some wind-up cosmic toy, some budding Lou Costello running through the abattoir
of his father's laughter to answer every hello with what he knew about *What's on second,*
Who's on first, the Watson family crick in his neck, his DNA, the queries growing louder
("What, Son? What, Son?"), the tom-tom golfing, clubbing in his head whenever anyone
acidulously said, "What's on your mind, Son? What is it, exactly?" "Nothing," Son said,
though he came to wish that everyone would hold the phone, would just drop dead,
or that, finally, at wit's end, Holmes would buy a clue, put a bullet through his head.
What is it fathers want? Someone to be in on it with, a coconspirator?
Someone to be included in insubstantial joy? Someone to be lorded over?
Or just someone so as not to be alone, spirit descending, to abandon, deride—
what son of a bitch? what son of mine?—some white sun day, some Whitsuntide?

Upon Reading that Abraham Lincoln Spent His Summer Nights as President
at a Cottage on the Grounds of the Soldiers' Home on the Outskirts of Washington
rather than at the White House, and that He and Edwin M. Stanton, His Secretary
of War, Spent the Better Part of One Evening in 1864 Freeing Two Peacocks
that Had Become Entangled in a Tree

Father Abraham and Stanton on their hands and knees, climbing trees, the war weighing
on them heavily, as if the sky itself were pressing down upon them, even denying birds
their rights, the peacocks, cock-robins, sky fallen, their feet tied with jute strings to wooden
blocks to keep them on the grounds, now tangled in the trees with the soldiers, the coffins,
the earth itself opening up again and again.

You can see it sometimes, a homestead family pulling up in a station wagon with Illinois
license plates at Walter Reed some night, good people. And you know they've driven all day,
sandwiches in the car, and they're getting out of the car the same way they would if they
were going to church. They're like brightly colored birds in the dim shadows of the evening
with the jute strings of their grief around their feet, as if they were dragging wooden
coffins to keep their hearts from flying away, as if they've tried to fly away so many times
that their hearts are permanently tangled in the trees now, each day growing more frantic,
more alone. Lincoln watches from his armchair, the white stone of his eyes, his heart
untangling them, emancipating them, setting their bird hearts free.

Love Field

There must be some conspiracy, some Warren Commission of love,

some Oliver Stone, grassy knoll, coup d'etat hit from above.

I will never believe again, will watch it all endlessly

on the History Channel, on reruns on late-night A&E,

my head snapping back like some Zapruder film of the dead,

love's Oswald, patsy, my blood running out ruby red,

blown away, like Jackie Kennedy in her bloodstained Barbie clothes,

standing next to Lyndon Johnson, the man with the bibulous nose,

one hand on the Bible to show his friends and his foes

that this is the way sometimes that it goes,

the other held up in the swearing-in pose

to show to the rest of the world that he knows

exactly what's going on. Nobody knows.

Poem to Be Read at 30,000 Feet

The plane went into the bay, like a rock, simple as that.

It dipped, plopped, chunked, like a sheep somehow dropped from the sky.

Or like the Golden Fleece lifted out from the dock, high over the Argo,

then the winch giving way, ergo, the way a star goes out, a faulty indicator light.

The pilots must have gone blind in the swarming fog, the camisoled night,

each one just before impact, smithereens, like the two boys they used to be,

each having gone into his parents' closet in the dark, into the mystery,

each trying on the long coat of the father, wide-eyed. Each passenger

on the hook as well, bloody ignorant (of so much, the bright arc of their lives,

the ocean's blinding swell), before they went in, sluicing like a cormorant,

before they were pole-axed, bollixed, Pollocked to the underside.

Look at them. One in the midst of wiping the mote from his eye, fully engaged.

One popping her ears. One finding her shoe. One coughing, mid-sentence,

mid-litote, his company, his high hopes sadly in arrears. One gazing, dully,

at a travel magazine. One blissfully asleep, mouth open as the sun's.

Another hung over, hammered, hands to his head. All of them, fore and aft,

like shepherds sore afraid amid angels floating above them, regal and daft,

none of them knowing what their lives had come to, each breath a permanent

fatal error, a malfunction of surprise and demands. None of them knowing

they were made from the stars, none of them knowing how remarkable you are,

what you mean to me (Lover, Dear Reader), how you hold this poem like my face

in your hands, each of us drifting through the fog to the sea.

Man Drowns

Nine a.m., and already I have heard again and again
about the man who drowned in his car yesterday when the Merrimack
overflowed after nine straight days of rain, the newscasters, Jack and Jane,
their endless spin, the cycle repeating, the *back in a minute*, the *yack yack yack*.
Hector Fuentes, fifty-nine years old, trying to get to work, they said,
thought he could make it, got caught in the middle, got over his head,
the scroll at the bottom, the loop coming round again to prove he is dead,
the news cam, the I-team, the eye-in-the-sky traffic helicopters circling about,
the white car in the water, its door still open like a pocket emptied out.
What told him to try it, that he needed to be at his desk, in his harness, his reins,
his boss, his father, the voice that taunted him, the river that flowed in his veins,
do the right thing, man up, pay down on the mortgage, easy enough,
buy his grandkids that swing, from which, if he pushed them high and hard enough
they could see the bright Merrimack roll by like a river of birds through the trees?
What had him out there, his life, the muck of it, suck of it, buckling his knees?
The man in the news, the Merrimack River deep in his lungs, what had him out there,
Hector Fuentes, fountain of sorrow, gasping for air?

Overflow

Strange to see this newly planted tree along this stretch of the Pike, its roadside coastal shelf,

a spruce, I think, slender, bottle-shaped, a coniferous Giacometti left to fend for itself,

as if the state had simply run out of funds, only one tree left, but green, Garcia Lorca green,

when suddenly, wondrous strange, as Horatio would say, I can see it again, a bottle of Teem,

twelve cents back then, and richly green, held out to me in the Templeton Pine Grove Cemetery

by Freddie Maahs, my dear best friend, who worked there with me after my father died.

And I would not take it from him, and he set it aside, and we raved and swore, and suddenly,

improbably, fought with each other, furious, green as we were. For a moment I think we tried

to make ghosts of each other, until just as suddenly we both sat down, bloodied, punch-drunk,

stupid, and out of breath, too tired to speak, beside the grave we should have been digging.

Then we thought for a while, he who sorely hated and was embarrassed by his beanpole drunk

of a father, and I who had simply lost my own, heart attack, and who had convinced myself

I would not take charity from anyone, and more than that, who did not have the 12 cents

to repay him, and who could not, would not, admit I was wrong, that I could see, even then,

it was just dumb love he was offering, shining, gleaming, standing right there on a gravestone,

like a bottle, green, beaded and cool, teeming with a comfort I was too stubborn to drink.

Witness

Predictable to some degree that a man with a red-and-white-striped stick-on umbrella hat
and a portable public address system bullhorn would be working the heart of Bourbon Street
in the name of the Lord. Telling all the jesters, masquers, Red Death revelers, that God
will not be mocked, that His patience is running out, that He sees us all, unblinking.
Predictable as well, perhaps, that his sidekick, his long-suffering Fortunato, would be hauling
a life-sized cross up the street with him on the Via Dolorosa, the road to the Superdome.

Less predictable the college kid, clean-cut, a Chuck Palahniuk *Fight Club* type,
having to be restrained, pulled away by his friends, physically lifted off the ground,
his feet moving in mysterious ways. Screaming at the Jesusers that they don't belong here,
that this is our holy place, our last sanctuary, that this is where we come for the sole purpose
of getting away from Jesus, that we should be free to mock God whenever we want,
that someone could get hurt tripping over a cross like that in the street,
that we should just be left alone, that we are all being crucified each and every day.
His friends haul him away, John the un-Baptist, God's true warrior in sackcloth and ashes,
His burning bush, His voice in the French Quarter wilderness, blessed troublemaker,
not to be scorned, not to be saved, crown-of-thorns-messiah of the way things really are.

Them Shoes

He says his name is Leon but it might as well be Earl

as he walks up to us on Bourbon Street betting he can tell every swinging boy and girl

among us exactly where we *got them shoes*. And we don't know much about Leon,

but we know one thing for sure, a sure bet when we see one,

despite the go cups we've had in our hands all afternoon, the Jesters, Mint Juleps, Hurricanes,

that there's no way Leon, or even Earl at that point, has the requisite brains

to divine where we got our Manolos or Tevas, what mall we went to, what store.

A few minutes later and we know a lot more,

including which pocket he's putting our money in,

the drinks wearing off, the weight of what's happened slowly settling in,

the world moving madly on, the lesson reverberating like a song on repeat,

as he says to us again and again, *You got them shoes on your feet.*

And we know as well that somehow we wanted him to do it, that we were betting to lose,

against the house, betting that he really did know where we got our Jimmy Choos,

that Leon in his *FEMA, My Ass* puffy baseball hat, mesh shirt, unlaced Pumas, followed us,

parked his car at the mall outside Nordstrom's because God told him to, to watch over us,

like some shoe angel, some Ninth Ward Elijah, some shepherd in gym shorts following a star,

that if we'd looked we could have seen God, at least His shoes, known exactly where they are.

Elvis, 1955

Idol already, in Memphis at least, before we got all shook up,

before we loved him tender, learned we could be cruel to a heart that was true.

When he walked into the matinee, sky-blue sportcoat, lady on his arm,

a minute or two after the movie had begun, even the usherless shadows knew

they could not save him. The audience saw their silhouettes glisten and sway,

like coming attractions in Cinemascope, movie within a movie, play within a play.

As the credits rolled they rose like the multitudes, blessed, reborn, with their remnants

of Dr. Peppers, popcorn, Jujubes, and followed him beaming into the light.

Outside a young woman, warm in a white cotton dress, walked toward him, reached out,

and touched him on the arm. "Cut me loose, cat," he said, lifting his hand,

and she fainted dead away, enraptured, spread out on a lawn, as if she were baptized,

as if she'd been loved and left by the Lord. Who wouldn't have believed,

if he had turned and said to go back to our homes, our lives,

that he couldn't be touched, that he had not yet entered into paradise?

**On the Occasion of My Two-Year-Old Granddaughter's First Attempts
at an Elvis Impression, I Recall the Difficulties of Her Birth**

When the syndicate doctors took us aside to say earnestly, insistently,
in the way that syndicate doctors are instructed to say, in that sibilant whisper
that comes unbidden, that my wife and I should not offer hope, not so much,
should be aware that the baby, if delivered, might not survive,
that our daughter, stitched up, cerclaged, should not drink from that cup,
should not get to believing, should know instead that this child might be damaged at best,
we held on, earnest in our own way, in the way we had come to believe.

And when my daughter went down on the intensive-care floor, the way a tree bends
in the face of a storm, the way a woman bends to wash a man's feet with her hair,
when she writhed with medication, shaken to her core, convinced in her way
that love could be that cruel, that she could be the engine of her daughter's demise,
her tremors generating the contractions that would kill her, we held on,
convinced that love would tender us, would hold us tenderly too.

And when the nurses came to us, one by one, over time, in the way
they have instructed themselves to do, in their secret, shared alliance,
each driven to believe that the heart can hold on, each of them saying,
Fatima-like, in their own sense of what it takes to be divine,
each of them nodding like a chorus, like backup singers, saying again and again
that the baby would be fine, the baby would be fine, we held on.

And this girl-child, this hey baby, fully present in the blue suede world,
runs now, all shook up, in some hound-dog dervish, some jailhouse-rocking circle of joy,
from the phone, around the kitchen again, and back to the phone,
saying, *Hey Baby, Hey Baby, Thankyouverymuch, Thankyouverymuch.*

II   . . . crawling between . . .

At the Optometrist's Office

CNN is always on. The old people seem to like it, the receptionist would say,

the way the stories loop around again, always the same, the pretty news anchor,

the weather in Missouri heading our way. But today something is happening,

live footage unfolding. The old people lean in, held in its sway.

They beheaded those soldiers, I hear one of them say, and then again, in the way

old people say everything twice, a loop come around again, *Those soldiers,*

those boys, they beheaded them. And now we all look, again and again,

except the receptionist, who never looks up, who hates her day-to-day, the rest of us squinting

at the scroll that keeps running at the bottom of the screen, like a free eye exam, each letter

showing up like an apple on a table, like a head upon a platter, the thing we have seen

since the day they were captured, the thing we keep seeing even when we look away,

the thing that keeps us staring at the thing that isn't there, the thing we can't imagine,

even with our eyes wide open, even if we walked outside, took to the street, holding

each other gently by the arm, even if trucks were driving by dragging the boys' bodies,

headless and harrowed, around and around the doctors' offices, the pretty news anchor,

the weather behind her, the thing we keep looking at, the thing we can't see.

Night Rain

My wife asks, upon rising, if I heard it coming down hard last night, the rain.
And I say I did not, though I saw, upon rising, the beads, the pearls of rain left
like dolphins' teeth, like little worlds along the eaves. And I wonder where I was, so deep
in sleep, so far away, as if I were absent, home from school one rainy 7th-grade afternoon,
not really sick, just lonely some, my classmates in arithmetic or doing penmanship,
the Rinehart system, their lonely heads in a row like raindrops on the line, consigned, bereft,
their loops, their little l's and o's, their curly q's, their pencils wearing down to nubs, the line
to use the sharpener, the shavings piling up inside like pillows filling up with down,
the long walk back between the rows, the little red-haired girl in the seat in front of mine,
mine empty all day long, so quiet-filled, her missing me a little, her pencil box upon
her desk, her plastic sharpener beside the inkwell hole, darkness-filled, where older students
long ago once dipped their feathered pens, goose-quilled, into India ink so dark and deep,
rich and still, to spill their lives along the pale blue, endless line like time, night rain
coming down hard already while we weren't listening, while we were fast asleep.

After the Reading, Driving Back to Massachusetts with Jim Beschta,
I Think of the Men Who Hold the World in Their Hands

Last night coming down from New Hampshire in a haze of Jameson and Iris Dement,
I remembered in fourth grade geography the multicolored Rand McNally map
of the world, the pink and yellow countries, the snowy polar caps, how I used to believe
that everything south of wherever we were had to be all downhill,
as if the northern hemisphere had an embargo on altitude,
as if the reason the South had lost the war was because they had to go uphill
at Little Round Top, as if when you were headed for Florida on vacation
after you pulled out of South of the Border, you and your brothers wearing sombreros
like floppy flowerpots lined up in the backseat, your father could just shut the engine off
if he wanted and light up a Camel, and you could have coasted all the way to Disney World,
the warm wind wafting through the open windows into the back of the car,
the wind lifting your sombreros a little, working its way out the window again,
huffing and puffing, all the way uphill to North Carolina.

And I remembered Atlas holding the world on his shoulders, the toughest job
in the world, no bathroom breaks, no days off, and wondering where he was standing
while he was doing that, and why in science class they never mentioned him at all,
the world on a wire in some kind of parabola, with all the other planets, and even
    the moon.

And you mentioned your daughter in Africa treating children with AIDS,
and I thought of my daughter flying to Geneva tonight coming down through the fog,
and we were two men rolling downhill in the mist and the rain of southern
   New Hampshire,
our daughters alone, beyond our reach, neither of us able to wrap our arms around
    the world,

our lives headed south, each of us in a kind of parabola broken off from the wires,

falling farther and farther away from the moon.

And we spoke of men wiring explosives to their bodies

to blow themselves bright as the sun, and men in the White House,

men in the war rooms with Rand McNally maps of the world on the walls,

men in the Middle East, the wind wafting up from southern Iraq,

and the two of us crossing into Massachusetts, all downhill from here.

Sleep Comes to Mary Todd Lincoln

Mary Todd, Mary Todd, one more letter than the name of God,
attack, attack, the taunt she heard behind her back from the very same people
who now stand and applaud, who dutifully nod to her and her husband
when they enter the theater box. Now God Himself will not let her sleep.
He talks and talks. When she slips away she is not of this age. She dreams
some future dream, some flickering screen, a movie, not a play, some
simpering comedy, some little man, not Booth, *Sic semper tyrannis!*,
the black hole of his mouth not synchronized fully with the image on the scrim,
not him, but a woman in Dallas crawling out on the back of a moving carriage,
to gather something. Flowers? Her marriage? The bits of her husband's brain?
She sleeps just like a funeral train, fits and starts, coming in and out of the rain.
She diffuses, becomes each raindrop on the windowpane, each a tear, a little planet,
a new nation of housewives all alone, crying in their sleep, *Mary Todd, Mary Todd,*
all Mary Todds now, and Lincoln is gone, and their husbands are blown up
by roadside bombs. They are led by little men who speak knowingly of God,
held hostage by theatrical, collateral harangue. They live sleepless like collapsed stars,
in their astral madhouses, their own little booths. They wait for the next big bang.

Driving Back from Crotched Mountain, Winter Storm, New Year's Eve

The man in front of me—what's he *doing?*—pulls over, no signal, to the side of the road,
gets out, begins sloughing his way, stooped and bent against the wind, to what I presume
is his driveway winding up and around the small box of a cabin which is his home.
He is waving me around, annoyed somehow, his left arm swooping low above the snow
in a way no man younger than himself would wave someone around, as if he'd been a soldier
or farmer all his life, as if he lived a little closer to the ground, his arm a sweeping scythe,
as if it were his holy job to wave the world to go around, as if he were my father, consigned
instead of hell to Peterborough, New Hampshire, where it turns out it always snows,
where he'd have to shovel the length of his driveway before his car would even have a prayer
of making it up the hill, and where he'd know the minute he finished, when all the clouds
had piled themselves like drunken sheep into the darkest corner of his day, the town would
come and plow him in again, as if he were Brueghel's eternal herdsman, his thick black oxen
never reaching town, all the steady, nervy peasants passing him by, heading to a festival,
some Candlemas of earth's delights, even Icarus dropping in, everyone in a lather,
the milkmaids and butcher boys, all cruddy and hopeful, thinking love—what else?—
is waiting for them just up the road, the man—what is his *problem?*—waving them ahead.

Brief History

> Ice-storms do that.
> Robert Frost

The town says it will send out crews to pick up all the broken branches from the storm
if we stack them neatly in clumps by the side of the road. And where they will take them
only God, the highway department, and Robert Frost can know, they so accustomed
to walking through town, frequenting the places we go to when we must, where we take
all our dead, the places we forget and then drive to in the spring, not fully awake,
moved and unmoved, turning down each tree-lined lane, not sure which one to take.
But this remove is more than poem or prayer. We build cairns, wickiups, mausoleums
of maple, birch, and pine, until the street is lined with stacks of limbs like stanzas, psalms.
No thicker than six to eight inches they say, more than the rule of thumb, the maximum
the width of the paperback my father gave me the day before he died, *The Pocket History
of the World*, the poor man's version of the eleven volumes of *The Story
of Civilization* by Will and Ariel Durant. And this too is a poor man's history,
all run together, repeating itself, this clearing, all of it, the wreckage, dross, the gory
dreck of all our willed and arieled past; here what could be the Eve tree in the garden,
here this woven vine like Cleopatra's golden bracelet clasp, here this broken,
shattered shaft driven deep into the ground like Brutus's blade, or Chingachgook's
into Magua's chest, and there this angled branch come to rest in a treetop like a Zero gone
down over Mindanao, the dead pilot stuck in the cockpit, no getting him out, so much
gone to hell on the ground already, the heavier trunks sectioned, sawed into lengths, each
the size and weight of a body at Little Round Top, Khe Sanh, Bastogne, the Somme.
I carry them deep enough into the woods to become what it is they will become.
I heft each one, gauge the changing landscape of my life amid the bracken, debris.
I hold my dead father in my arms. I think of him, his brief history,
how he would love to be here now, to come back from whatever broken place he is in.
It is broken here too. He would be right at home. I am more alone than I have ever been.

For the Man with the Erection Lasting More than Four Hours

He's supposed to call his doctor, but for now he's the May King with his own Maypole.

He's hallelujah. He's glory hole. The world has more women than he can shake a stick

at. The world is his brickbat, no conscience to prick at, all of us Germans he can *ich*

lieber dich at. He's Dick and Jane. He's Citizen Kane. He's Bob Dole.

He's Peter the Great. He's a czar. He's a clown car with an extra car.

Funiculi, Funicula. He's an organ donor. He works pro boner. He's folderol.

He's fiddlesticks. He's the light left on at Motel 6. He's free-for-alls.

He's Viagra Falls. He's bangers and mash. He's balderdash. He's a wanker.

He's got his own anchor. He's whack-a-doodle. King Canoodle. He's a pirate, Long John

Silver, walking his own plank. He has science to thank. He's in like Flynn. He's Gunga Din,

holding his breath, cock of the walk through the valley of the shadow of death. He's Icarus,

hickory dickorous, the mouse run up the clock. He's shock and awe. He's Arkansas.

He's the package, the deal, the Good Housekeeping Seal. He's Johnson and Johnson.

He's a god now, the talk of the town. He's got no place to go but down.

Upon Reading that a Noisy Cloth Factory Separated the Family Homes
of Sandro Botticelli and Amerigo Vespucci

Little Barrel, they called him, beautiful layabout, lazy angel, though Sandro was passive,

dreamy, paintbrush thin. "Paints when he wants to," his father proclaimed. "Why can't

you be more like Vespucci?" he cried, "Discover a country, get out of the house?"

All night across the street Vespucci's mad mother crying out for her son, all alone

in his barrel-shaped boat, *"Amerigo, Amerigo,"* his name like a vine encircling the world.

All day the cloth factory, the threading machines, wooden contraptions, clackety-clacketing,

cocking, shuttling, warping, weaving. How could one sleep? What dreams would go there?

When asked, years later, why he never married, Sandro said he dreamed about it once

and grew so terrified that he left the house, sailed the drunken streets until morning arrived.

Vespucci all this time on the palette of the ocean, the mainsails flapping like triptychs

in the breeze, sudden America spread out before him, naked, silent, an odalisque continent.

Back home Botticelli, writhing to the rhythm of the spreaders, the shuttles, his mind spinning

out of control, Mars versus Venus, Jacob wresting his Angel to bless him, betides,

until his own angels appeared at the touch of his hand, their rivers of hair threaded gold,

his canvas their haven, their bright heaven on earth, stepping out of their half shells,

their own little barrels, onto seas of shimmering paint, skeins of silent cloth,

each woman the New World of his dreams.

On Bethlehem's Plain

They are sending her home for Christmas, back to Nickel Mines,

the last of the Amish girls hospitalized in the shootings.

She will ride all the way in the ambulance from Philadelphia,

look out the window past the blue reversed caduceus, the serpent and staff,

see the holiday travelers, the last-minute shoppers, the exits backed up at the malls.

She will look, unblinking, at the other children, grim, who will look back at her

from the rusty, elongated church vans with names like Hope and Free and Grace Evangelical.

She will see the pale school buses lined up in the lots, empty as barns in the spring.

She will see the convoys of soldiers, hunters in trucks, then the long, feathered fields,

the different grasses, still green somehow, the weather so warm. She will see the shepherds,

the horse carts, and the walkers, like Sadducees, their beards lifting up in the wind.

She will see the school's been torn down. She will close her eyes but she will see it still,

the single room she continues to attend, the blood on the walls like holly.

She is coming to us, and she knows everything, the child coming back to be born.

She will never believe. She will not believe kings, will not wish on any scattered star.

She has seen a few things. She knows who we are.

Look, Look

In the grainy news footage an old woman in a bathing suit standing on a beach.
Overweight. Heavyset. Seen from behind. Suit too small. European.
Not the way an old woman should be seen, we say. We look anyway,
first with disdain, then dollops of pity, in the way we have come to look.
We say Cover yourself. You are no longer young. We say the world is always looking
at our bottoms. We consume her, spit her out, the woman and the others looking out
at the ocean. Then we see it too, what has them up looking, what they must have seen
first as cloudbank horizon, until they saw it truly, until it rushed at them spitting,
tsunami, tsunami, the god of a wave that was coming to kill them.

The image turns over like a bird in a loop, like a photograph tumbling all night underwater,
then come to the light, this old woman on a beach. She is all the old women we have seen
and forgotten, like paintings we have passed on our way to another, aunts who have died,
Mother Courage, Kathe Kollwitz, relatives distant as trees overseas. But she does not turn,
the woman on the beach, nor do the others. They look at the wave, sun-filled, that is coming
to eat them, bigger, whiter than anything they've ever seen. They do not run, not yet, caught
in the web of their looking, the way shepherds must have looked at the angels above them,
struck dumb, agog, the way we all look sometimes at the world that loves us and kills us,
the world that bamboozles, flim-flams, Dick and Janes us again and again, crying, Look, Look,
this world that keeps coming, this world we behold even to the cup of our deaths overflowing
and still never fully believe, this fleshy, ancient, crepuscular world, this old woman on a beach
who turns, opens her arms, runs to us screaming, asking nothing but all of our love.

For Lou Bishop, the Drunk Who Lived up the Road

We always heard you made it to the show, the Pirates, I think, a cup of coffee at least,

enough perhaps to have heard some lug in the bleachers yelling like a bona fide fool

after you legged out a triple, *Lou, Lou*. But when I looked for you in *The Baseball*

Encyclopedia, after finding a forerunner of my dead friend Bill Holshouser

(Herm, righty, reliever for the Cards, 0 and 1 lifetime, 7.80 ERA), you weren't there,

no sign of you at all, though I can see you still, walking back and forth to the Hubbardston

packy, bags in hand, your land overgrown, your little house, your mangy dog,

all of us scared to go near your yard, the neighborhood bogeyman, stubbled, silent,

lanky in your holey, baggy pants, our own Boo Radley, Abe Lincoln gone bad.

Sometimes on our way home from school we'd find you lying in a ditch,

mumbling God's holy glossolalia to yourself, too drunk to get to your feet.

We'd jump at first, mark you from a distance, as if you were a porcupine, spooked,

as if we were spelunkers and you the Mammoth Caves, or we the Hardy Boys,

you the bastard son of John Wilkes Booth, as if you'd leap at us with a rusty sword,

yelling *Sic semper tyrannis*, if we got too close, as if there were some posted reward.

Off and on we wondered why they didn't teach these things at school,

how people got like this, though we all had fathers, harried and cruel,

and all of us knew the ones among us who got into trouble, moved away,

the ones sent to reform school, the kid who wore the same shirt every day,

the one they grabbed by the scruff of the neck, the one who came away

from the principal's office and never said a word, though his eyes had turned

to gold or gray, the short straw, tough nut, bad seed, the one they consistently drew

for us as object lesson, parable boy, *Lou, Lou*, the wrath of what could happen to us,

the sum of our lives, what we, if we fell along the way, could end up amounting to.

Oh, Lou, Lou, they murdered you, you poor son of a bitch. And we loved you then,

we loved you true, though we never even knew that we knew, scared half to Jesus,

half to death. Sometimes when the moon is strangled blue by the nimbus of our lies,
I think you're still running, hustling, half out of breath, deep in the dugout dreams
of your grave. I hope you're taking them deep, that they're stomping somewhere,
that you can hear them roar and clap and rave and sigh, *Oh, my,* that somebody's
giving you a 'Gansett, that somehow you know, despite what they say,
that we all have our encyclopedia page, our time to come, our time to go,
that everybody, everybody makes it to the show.

History

The first day of spring
and the women who live next door have gotten back together again.
The one who moved away unpacks the things she took with her six months ago.
We watched her then. We watch her now, our hands at the window,
the way that neighbors gauge and stare, the way we make our history.
We log each item recovered, note each trivet, each sorry chair,
all back where they started, their rightful place. We remember the endless row,
the splay of rubbish bags she left back then like black plastic frogs at the end of the yard,
and the ratty cartons, the water-stained boxes from the flood they had the year before
leaning into each other, clumped and off-balance, filled with all they had rummaged through,
their tattered history. That, and the sad-eared, reddish rubber plants, the yucca, ficus, spiders,
dead for months, of blight, like scarecrows lost, the happenstance, the truck of our lives.
Finally, oddest of all, the Barcalounger, orange, brown, white, left like an uncle, totally
surprised, half in and half out of the road at the end, as if to invite anyone who wanted
to sit for a while, take a load off, before the rubbish men came, taking each item,
lifting them soundlessly, democratically, without bias or claim, tossing them
into the curved and humpbacked maw of the truck, each one hurled
like Jonah into beluga, baleen, the future, the past, the raw open mouth of the world.

And she has brought back the boy they had made, three and a half now, towheaded, tall,
and he stands at the center of his new and old lawn, sticks out his stomach and wails
at the world. One word all he says, again and again, a Johnstown Flood, a Babylon,
a word of such weight we can't make it out, a lost friend's name perhaps, history now,
or the name for the home he has left and the one he's come back to that he missed once
before, his home like the moon he can see now, still there in the blue of this morning.
He wails in the way one would cry for a doll left for good on a train, or a dog gone off
that will never return. He's got us all at the windows again,

our fingers held up to the lace as if we were saints bestowing a blessing,

or women in history so lost in their curtained time, and ours, they are drawn

to the light that comes like milk to the window, like the milky maids of Vermeer,

or the way a young woman in prison at three a.m. wakes to the blue and vermilion

ambulance lights flashing in the courtyard, the reflection circling, looping again

and again on her ceiling and cell walls like a kaleidoscope, a prism,

a skein made of silence and fear.

And now he is crying louder than ever, like a little boy Buddha, fat-bellied, strong.

He has lost everything, his mouth filling up with all of his sorrow, the song of his diphthongs

and leftover vowels, crying *Om, Om*, or *Home, Home*, until his two mothers

come out to take him inside, calming him, soothing him, saying *There, There*.

And suddenly I know what my father was saying when I was a child,

as he pointed so wildly to the treeline, the brake at the edge of the clearing,

There, There, the albino deer and the fawn that came one night and stood,

skitterish, thin, white as the clouds that skimmed the edge of the moon,

their eyes in our flashlight haloes like the bright lost stars of our lives.

How they stood there for a moment waiting for us to speak.

How we wished that we knew some word full of grace, some word

that would bring them closer to us. Night after night after that he went out

to see if they would come back, and he searched for that word for the rest of his life,

some word he could say for what he believed, what he thought might be true,

some place he might find, some unsayable word for the nub of the future,

which turns always and irremediably into the beautiful trash we call history,

which Napoleon said wonderfully was the collection of lies we agree to believe in,

the place my father could see and hold like a chalice and still never say, never give to us,

the word that it takes all our lives to make clear, the word they both are saying now, my father and the boy with two mothers standing in the yard on the clearest spring day

of their lives, the moon and the stars still there in the sky like the deer at the edge

of the clearing, and some bird high above all of us now, the yellow-tailed hawk of our history,

the bird that has watched us every day of our lives, and which at night we think is a star,

lazily circling with each loop, with each scree, with each caw, the bird inside the husk

of the bird, the bird we carry in the blood of our hearts, our hearts that we lug

from one place to the next, the lost luggage of our lives, always moving, being stored,

the word that was in the very beginning, the host of our bodies in the mouth of the Lord.

Throwing Out the Marriage Bed

Day after Christmas, our headboard, frame, and bureau mirror of nearly forty years
propped atop our rubbish bags, like Huck and Jim's lean-to aboard their errant raft,
or Noah's wayward ark, the mirror like a solar window, useless now for forty days.
When they come, our garbage men, crisscrossing, Carhartted, one darker than the other,
they know without speaking they will have to come together to get the lifting done,
their hands knowing exactly what to do, the solid oak spindles settling evenly, cleanly,
within the mouth of the truck. It is as if they are married, these two, have been for years,
like the paired moving men who, sweating and moaning, pushed and pulled the new bed
up the stairs yesterday, and who said in unison, smacking their hands, that it would last us
a lifetime, then looked at us like children, awed, as if they had said something profound
by accident, like cavemen discovering the fire of speech after dragging something home,
or EMTs with ADD, carrying heavy death into the house by mistake, who would have to
take it back out again now. We do not have a lifetime. The bed will outlive us,
the weight of it alone enough to keep us in this place, Penelope, delivered Odysseus,
olive tree as corner post. This is the bed we will die in, perhaps, each in our time, the one
neither of us will live to see lifted from the street, however carefully, even gently, like water
spilling slowly over a dam at the break of day. Look now, how they tender the mirror
into the open bay, how it fills with the light of the moving, diluvial world.

Teachers

When Miss Sokoloski, our first-year French teacher, leaned over her desk to get out

our quizzes from the lower-right-hand drawer, we all leaned with her, even the girls, to see

that softness and shadow under the scoop neck of her Jackie Kennedy two-piece suit.

Dumb as we were we knew she was too sweet to teach French, too pretty as well. When she

went to the board we studied declensions we never even knew that we had. When she cried

one day because some of us cheated, none of us could say in any language, Romance or not,

that it was because she was so beautiful. A year later she left and we figured she married,

someone fluent in French who loved her like we did, *tout de suite* and tongue-tied. And when

Mr. Burke, Junior English, who looked like Gregory Peck in *To Kill a Mockingbird* and wore

the same suit three times a week, slumped in his seat and would not speak when the PA

announced JFK had been killed, he taught his best lesson, that we all lived somewhere

between what was right and what was wrong, that beauty lived right in the middle,

that teachers felt the same thing we all felt too, they just kept it inside like a test in a drawer.

And we thought if only he could marry Miss Sokoloski, read poems all night and translate

each other, but she was too pretty and he was too poor. My teachers, all dead now or pretty

close to it, like Jackie, the Kennedys, and Marilyn Monroe, who knew everything once,

except what they taught us, the tests that were coming, the things we would know.

News

Pictures are hung. People are hanged, Ms. Novak proclaimed,
as she tapped on the board, demanding that we write that down.
Novak the Slovak we called her, but we all wrote it down,
except for the Jefferson brothers playing hangman in the back,
the ones she invited to drop by for a while after school.
Detention for inattention, she said, as their necks snapped back
and their eyes rolled up in their heads. *People are hanged.*
Last week Saddam in his jumpsuit refusing to be hooded, taunted,
haranguing his tormentors. And today as well, the former chief judge
of the revolutionary court, and Saddam's half-brother, former head
of the secret police, his head snapping completely off, the drop charts
all wrong, the grim machinations of weight, gravity, and momentum
skewed, the rope swinging freely like a rat tail through the gallows
trapdoor, the hangmen in their full-face balaclavas, lever brothers,
cleaned out now, empty-handed, unemployed for a while. And the boys,
world brothers, nine- and ten-year-olds, one in Texas, one in Pakistan,
dead this week, having jumped from their bunks, having studied
the video, having been attentive, their bodies so still, like a picture, hung.

Lisbon

A man has been yelling since midnight in Lisbon, yelling nonstop for an hour or so
this hot August night, the windows all open all over the city, from Rua de Sao Paolo
to the top of Bairro Alto. He is screaming at the top of his lungs in his kitchen, some song,
some language I cannot imagine, some sad fado singer gone mad at rehearsal, gone loco,
basso profundo, the others all dumbstruck in their sad pantaloons, his tirade so piercing,
his song a great wound. Even the roosters are wide awake listening. I think it's his daughter
to whom he is speaking, his daughter home late on this long Friday night. He is hectoring her
about fathers, tradition, that she has disgraced him, her family, her country, his voice pleading
more than anything, quivering, shaking, his urging so true that it stills all the neighbors.
Not one says, *Shut up! We all need our sleep.* Not one says, *Be quiet. Our daughters
are with us.* If anything they would come in pajamas and nightshirts to stand at his window
to applaud for his aria. *Saudade*, they would say, the sadness of things, his voice breaking
for the fathers and daughters of Lisbon, the love they've been given that must not be lost. So
his daughter sings too in her silence, her dreaming, the song of the boy she left standing,
how he aches to be with her, how his song will be true. Now the father grows weary. Soon
he will sleep, a cathedral caved in, an earthquake undone, his voice gone as soft as the moon.
He wanders offstage, cues night to come on, having waited in the wings like a rose,
to sing to each heart in the city of Lisbon, to sing the one song that everyone knows.

Sirhan Sirhan

The double name, the name said twice,

as if saying it once would not be enough, would not suffice,

the way sweet Swedes, Norwegians named their sons, giving names like advice,

Johnny Johnson, Lars Larson, Oley Olsen, each name its own silhouette,

its own shadow, so they'd find their way home, so they wouldn't forget,

wouldn't be bewildered by life, by its double-edged welter, its echo of pain,

by the call of the wild, by Brandon de Wilde calling *Shane, Shane,*

the way we cried *Bobby, Bobby*, thinking we could bring him back again,

the way blood pooled like an aura, *the horror, the horror*, around his head,

as if grace were a place you had to say twice, the last hammer strokes on a nail driven dead,

like *Paw Paw, Walla Walla, Sing Sing*, or Pacino yelling *Attica, Attica*, for all of us to see.

Sirhan Sirhan, when he closes his eyes, amen, amen, when he prays for the truth he can see,

sees the single words, the words we say once: *life, death, day, night, peace, home, free.*

The Grief Counselor's Day Off

Goes for walks, but it's no use. Grief everywhere, shooting up her nose, slicing her hair.

The school bus goes by. Kids screaming in rows. She knows there's a kid in there

lost inside his baggy clothes, and another in the middle somewhere where he grows

even more invisible, another with her mother's pills, another cutting 666 and X's and O's

into the fake leather of the seat in front of him. The girl to his left, her honeyed hair

hiding her face, stares at her arm. Then another bus, bright as a bee, stops, goes.

She walks into the woods past the playing fields. She's been there before,

past the condoms and beer cans where the weekend bonfires roar,

past the burned-out place where the kids aren't allowed to go anymore,

to the hollowed-out tree that she visited last May

where the quarterback hanged himself because he was gay.

There's a beehive in the hollowed part, perfectly gray,

and the bees go in like buses at the end of the day,

each one coming in, rumbling, pulling away.

She hears their thousand-winged song, each sweet word that they say.

She wants to warn them there'll be this bear someday

that will ravage them, rip at their lives, tear them away,

but the bees tell her gently, in their own busy way,

not today, not today, not today.

Finding My Dead Father at the Worcester Art Museum

Forty years now, but, Jesus, here he is, seen, unseen,
in George Bellows's "Monhegan Island, 1913,"
these rocks, splashed red and green with sea moss, spiky grass,
so like the rocks he stood on in a photo with his brother Bobby, on a weekend pass
in Gloucester, 1943, before being killed in the war, plane crash. My father
holding out his hand, palm up to the sky, the photo staged, Bobby standing further
out on the rocks, looking tiny, like a toy, as if he were perched on my father's hand,
my father lecturing him like Gulliver, telling his Lilliputian little brother to listen up, stand
and deliver, watch his step, telling him from that moment on how things were going to be.
But whoever took the picture didn't get it right, a tiny space between Bobby's feet
and my father's hand, as if Bobby were floating in a painting by Magritte,
as if he were dead already, disconnected, ascending into heaven, to some angular grace,
my father, dead wrong but still trying, telling him to stay put, to stay in this place.

Both gone now, great and small, seen, unseen,
these crashing waves, these rocks, these bellows, red and green,
my hand stretched out, my heart so full, this empty, hollow, delivered sea,
how near, how far, how things are going to be.

III   . . . in your philosophy . . .

Girl on the People Mover

This girl, eighteen perhaps, driving the airport's motorized cart,

the one that beeps through the terminal like the plague bell, endless,

like the heart. Her cart is empty for the moment. She drives with one hand.

With the other she twirls her dyed and braided hair. She moves the strand lightly,

slowly, instinctively, both with and without great care. Within the next minute

her headset will blare, and someone, a mother perhaps, a woman gone weary

with the weight of the walking world, will need to be moved, will sit for a while,

Isis-proud, regal as she will ever be, her handbag resting evenly just above her knees,

her subjects walking alongside her and then behind, empress of the end of the world.

And she, the driven one, will come to know, vaguely, while being moved,

that her life is all but over. Already she can see, as if from Gericault's Medusa raft,

the River Jordan, the other shore, and this girl, brazenly unaware, coming toward her

twirling her burnished and goldenized hair. But for now, for just this moment,

the girl remains alone, moved and unmoved, her gaze free to lift out where it wants,

somewhere further off, far away, raised up somehow, some shimmering oasis of air

both on the horizon and just a little bit above. Her life is over too. She is in love.

Cross-Country

The kid running last as the team heads through town during afterschool practice,
so far behind all the others he's lost them completely, in his own time zone,
his own ecosystem. They're at the halfway already, the drive-thru Dunkin' Donuts
by the Unitarian church that's been closed for a year. They'll make the turn en masse,
like some Christo running fence, head back toward the gym, pass him on the way,
say they ordered him a mocha Dunkaccino, the kid still running to catch them,
the one with no art, no rhythm, his arms swinging sideways into the wind, running
like a drunk holding onto a tree, running toward his father and away from him too,
hunched in his running, Quasimodo, contrapposto, running in his agony, stitch in his side,
Pheidippides at Marathon, or pure St. Sebastian, his pincushion heart, or sweet John Keats
running up the Spanish Steps, heart in his hand, coughing his lungs out for his love,
Fanny Brawne, the kid running in water, running in molasses, running like a bastard,
the kid we all know who is never going to get there, running for his life
right into the wall, the last shall be first, the best kid of all.

Yale

We stand under the balustrades
in the narrow nave of a library entranceway,
proud parents, prospective students, tour guide,
stayed for a moment by that prim awkwardness
that befalls daughters and sons
forced to stand in such proximity
with the expectations of their families.

Suddenly, from an alcove a cleaning lady appears
pushing a blue plastic barrel on a cart with four wheels,
her pushbrooms and dustmops upright and proud in their slots.
She stops for a moment. We are all in her way.
Then she parts us like Moses in a sea of admissions,
and there is no name for the silence that begins to accrue,
no word for the Egypt of darkness that works in her eyes.

Our perky group leader asks if we have any questions.
No one asks if the cleaning lady gets to take evening classes.
No one asks if she qualifies for the legacy rule.
No one asks why her eyes will be all we'll remember, years from now,
two black stones, gleaming, on an African shore.
Someone asks about computers, about problems with roommates.
Someone asks about locks on the doors.

Saints

When Leadbelly sings "Down in the Valley" the man in the song is so low,

so forlorn, that he asks his lover to hear the wind blow,

to hang her head over and hear the wind blow.

He says if she doesn't love him, "to love whom you please,"

but to throw her arms 'round him, to give his heart ease.

He says he loves her so much even the angels in heaven know.

He says build him a castle forty feet high,

so that he can see her as she goes by.

And it's only at the end when he asks for some mail,

that he tells her to send it to the Birmingham jail.

Maybe jails serve to make some men saints.

Maybe saints are just lovers torn away from their love,

who find themselves singing when the moon breaks restraints,

climbs the forty-foot wall, heads for the angels above.

I think how Martin Luther King did time in the valley,

wrote letters of his own from the Birmingham jail,

and that's close enough to sainthood for me.

And when people say the word "saint" is too free,

that we use it too much, toss it around, liberally,

I say there are saints in supermarkets, angels in malls.

I say there are thousands of Peters and Pauls,

that the DPW man who at two in the morning hauls

dead deer off the roads, bleaches the blood, goes home to his wife,

holds the grail of the world in his hands. I say we are all saints, consigned for life,

locked up, doomed, each night to watch the searchlight moon come and go,

each day to awake, hang our head over, hear the wind blow.

Bootleg

It's a song called "Silver Mantis" that T Bone Burnett sings
on an old bootleg Bob Dylan CD from a Rolling Thunder Revue concert
down in Fort Worth, Texas, over thirty years ago. In the song,
which tells the tale of a lowly servant a thousand years ago
who saves the daughter of a Japanese warlord from a kidnapping,
but who then is thrown into the dungeon because the warlord is jealous and enraged,
Burnett makes a mistake, a minor one, simply transposing the name of the servant
for the name of the princess (the rough equivalent of a Shakespearean actress saying
"O Juliet, Juliet, wherefore art thou Juliet?"). And to the casual listener, or the uninitiated,
or the drunk or lazy, the moment in the song might go completely unnoticed, no harm
done either way, but to the devotee, the sentimental, or the lowly servants among us
(who are always in danger of being thrown into dungeons by our own rough equivalents
of warlords, jealous and enraged), it makes us love the song even more.

I say maybe T Bone was a little drunk or a little lazy that day.
Or maybe he was caught up in his own moment, maybe playing before the largest crowd
of his life because Dylan had loved the song too and had asked him to join the revue
(although even Dylan himself made mistakes, introducing the song with the wrong title
and mispronouncing the name of the Japanese princess).

Or maybe T Bone just knew somehow, like some silver mantis in his heart,
what all artists know over time, that art is one endless mistake after another,
that architects sometimes make intentional mistakes, turning the last piece of tile
upside down in the floor of ten thousand tiles to show no pride before the face
    of the Lord,
that the part of the song where the singer loses control is the heart's true song,
the essence of all that is holy in love, that lovers when they freely exchange their hearts

with the other exchange their names as well, that they know in the room they make

of their love that each name is sacred and the same, that Romeo is Juliet and Juliet is Romeo,

that the heart of a lowly servant can be the heart of a princess, that there's no mistake about it,

that love may be the greatest mistake of them all, the rough equivalent,

the bootleg version of the perfect song of our lives.

Mr. Muckle

I am teaching my four-year-old granddaughter about Mr. Muckle,
the deaf and blind man in the 1934 W. C. Fields movie *It's a Gift*, Mr. Muckle,
who along with being deaf and blind, is also a mean-spirited, cantankerous son of a bitch,
possessing none of the tender humility we've come to expect and even demand
from our deaf and blind men, Muckle, who white-sticks his way into Fields's hardware store,
first poking his cane right through one of the two glass front doors, then knocking over
and falling on twenty boxes of imported glassware, crushing them utterly, then imperiously
and without any regret whatsoever, ordering a pack of chewing gum, which he refuses to take
  with him, choosing instead to have it wrapped and delivered, and who then, agitated,
  waving his cane at the world, proceeds to destroy, one by one, an entire display of light
  bulbs, unwrapped, stacked individually, piled so high that no one, absolutely no one in
  his right mind or otherwise, would ever stack them that way, or go anywhere near them,
  or ever consider
even touching them, one bulb displaced causing them all to fall down, a slowly building
  cacophony of small explosions, one right after the other, bulb after bulb, wattage after
    wattage, popping into splinters, shattering like all the lost bright ideas of the world.
And I know already in my heart that this movie, ancient now, its humor so droll, so far
  removed from her world that it is like news from some alternate universe of comportment
and neglect, will make my granddaughter a little more odd or standoffish, a little more
vulnerable, a little more likely to be bullied or tormented with text messages in junior high,
a little bit more like the uppermost light bulb on an enormous pile of adolescent light bulbs
just waiting to be smashed and broken.

And it's not about laughing at a deaf and blind man. It's Fields who's the funny one, so beset by
  all his customers, a man demanding cumquats, a wife who's a shrew, an assistant on roller
    skates, molasses on the floor, Fields who's so flustered, so pointlessly caught up in wrapping
a package of bubblegum that he misgauges the oncoming danger, calling out to Mr. Muckle
as he sees too late the inevitability of it all, Muckle's cane swinging wildly, the endcap

of light bulbs like some fragile iceberg, Muckle a blind Titanic with a stick, Fields almost

singing as he cries out, repeatedly, "Look out, Mr. Muckle! Look out! Look out!"

as if Muckle could hear him, as if he actually could look out, and then, magically,

(there is no other word for it) Fields as his last resort calling him "Honey," the word

hanging in the air, as if that would help, as if some felicitous endearment would calm him,

stop him in his tracks, save the store from imminent disaster, or perhaps actually restore

Mr. Muckle's sight. But by then it's too late, Muckle strolling out, putting his cane perfectly

through the other glass front door on the way, then walking across Main Street through

crosstown traffic, cars, ambulances, even fire trucks, careening around him while

he blithely walks on, never missing a beat, the deaf and blind Fifth Horseman of the

Apocalypse wandering into the hinterlands, unseen, eternal, unscathed.

Ultimately, of course, it's not Fields or even Muckle I'm trying to teach you,

my granddaughter. It's the Apocalypse, the way we're all getting muckled each and every day,

the way it keeps coming for us, mean-spirited sometimes, deaf and blind to us all, waving

its white stick, unceremoniously knocking us down when we're not looking, when we're

just minding the store, when we lose sight momentarily of what's always coming for us,

what's trying, according to all the intransigent, indefatigable laws of Nature, to do nothing

less than kill us every day, the day that's been coming for us since the day we were born,

how we fail to appreciate, fail to propitiate, how we see it too late every time, how it might

have been appeased, a stick of gum held out, perhaps, some sweetness we had within us

that we could have offered all too easily, a simple word we could have said to the hellhounds,

the hellmouth awaiting us all, "Honey," perhaps, just the way, my dear, my little plum,

you might remember years from now your mother saying that word to your father once,

casually, almost blindly, "Honey," the word holding everything that ever brought them

and held them tenderly together, the glass doors of the life they had built for each other,

all their bright ideas, their glassware, the shimmering crystal of their dreams.

Upon Reading on a Flight from Atlanta the Latest Slang Term for the Act of Defecation

My wife and I begin to laugh, individually at first, then in tandem,

and then alternately, like Didi and Gogo, our own little Theatre of the Absurd.

We are caught short momentarily, set loose by the use of the phrase, each word

in its place, throats tight, faces flushed, and then, because we are on a plane, we become

aware, each seated on our little throne, our fitted chair, that others are listening, tittering,

and we laugh harder still, helpless now, like wedding guests, lit, so shit-faced drunk we are

howling now, so effulgent and contained we are a small country, a Liechtenstein of loopy

laughter. The flight attendant smiles at us, helplessly, a little afraid we will actually laugh

our asses off, trigger the seat cushions as flotation devices, the people around us now

laughing as well, a wispy, gassy rebellion, as if we were Canterbury pilgrims, horsing around,

on our way to some stand-up cathedral, some heaven of ha ha's and wheeze.

And how do we tell them, wiping our eyes, back up and start over,

our cacophonous offertory, our comic scatology, our laugh till we die?

We don't die. We shuffle, adjust, do as we must, dust ourselves off,

return to the serious world. We stifle ourselves, like accordions dying, like bellows

left open. A phrase all it was, for going to the bathroom, what kids say these days,

dipsticks and dillweeds, and we so much older, too old, each of us, to be laughing like this,

like geezers, like silverback fools. They say what we would say about taking a dump,

grunting one out, laying some cable, as if we were young again, as if we were cool.

They say it in perfect imitation of the parents they will become.

They say they have to drop the kids off at the pool.

Upon Seeing a Former Lover Pull Up Next to Me at the Intersection of Metaphysics Lane and Memorial Drive

What are the odds you would pull up alongside me in traffic,

your husband, stolid, handsome, blissfully unaware,

and you, languorous, lolling your arm out the window,

your Marlboro Light 100 dangling like my life,

your eyes like the sign for infinity?

Only slightly less likely than the vast mathematical chances

of Marilyn Monroe and Albert Einstein pulling up in a red Mini Cooper,

Marilyn beaming in her white dress, her legs on the dashboard,

Albert bemused, the wind like a theorem in his hair,

having come from some universe of physics and longing,

some world infinitely better than this one,

some cosmos where lovers go parallel parking,

a place they have found where love makes more sense,

where I could reach out, take your hand within my own,

say I love you forever before the wind picks up,

before your smile fades,

before the light begins to change.

Upon Reading a Poem Entitled "Upon Seeing a Former Lover Pull Up Next to Me at the Intersection of Metaphysics Lane and Memorial Drive"

If I say this really happened once, the audience swells with sardonic laughter, and I drive

home feeling like John Dunce, Cornpone Boy; or else it's greeted with the thick, sweet

silence that invariably awaits the utterances of the Truly Lovelorn and Hopelessly Put-Upon.

If I say it again, I get a free commemorative plaque and lifetime permanent guest pass

in the Country-Western Drive-Thru Dairy Queen 24-Hour Memorial Lovers-in-Hell

Hall of Fame and Farmers' Museum, next to the Pyramis and Thisbe Hole-in-the-Wall

Gang Members' Pavilion, and just a short drive from the Dante and Beatrice Hell-in-a-Hand-

basket Water Arcade, where kids toss quarters idly into the Big Rock Candy Mountain

Fountain-of-Tears, or hang alongside the Butterfly McQueen I Don't Know Nothin' Gone-

with-the-Wind-Tunnel to buy commemorative Paolo and Francesca bottles of Fresca,

seeing how they look so parched and all, their necks and backs so painfully arched, like

used to be Olympians, like lovers blown apart, then brought back alongside each other,

closer than hell but never quite touching, as if someone could derive pleasure from that,

like diagonal parking spaces in space, or a drive-in movie in separate cars, the stars out

and all, when you're thinking with the total assurance and logical precision of a drunken

sailor upon a runaway horse that you know what's what, that you could hold the sweet

moon in your arms, when everyone else knows clear as a Memphis belle that you've got no

pull at all, that you have the chance of a fish-fried Fourth of July snowball in hell, and just

when you figure that out for sure, she pulls away at the lights, the Just Married sign duct-

taped on the back, your heart tied to the bumper, bouncing down Memorial Drive

like a runaway trailer made of sneakers and old tin cans.

On Hardly Ever Hearing Anyone Say *Boy, Howdy* Anymore

for Bill Holshouser

Who knows more about the panic and ache,

the half-baked rolling thunder of the human condition,

than the moonies, the loonies, the krishnas and witnesses,

those long-suffering wanderers in their Sears & Roebuck suits,

door after door being closed in their faces?

Hell, Lassie would have chased them out of the yard,

Timmy and his family in rocking chairs on the porch,

laughing the way they did at the end of each episode.

Lot's wife would have shut them out too,

turning her back, salt on her tongue,

Jesus, Mary, and Joseph.

Even Jesus might have wondered about opening the door,

sitting quiet as hell in the reading room

of Joseph of Arimathea's cave

when they came like angels and rolled the stone away.

Most likely He'd have lit out for the territory

when they had given up and crossed the street,

His copy of *The Watchtower* sticking up in the mailbox

like a drowning man's hand,

like a rattler on a fencepost when the river overflows.

I knew a man once who got up from the game, opened his door to a couple of witnesses,

wild-eyed, dreamy, Scotch tape on their glasses, scuffs on their shoes.

He accepted a pamphlet, then asked for them all, said he knew that his friends

would all want one too, took them in a clump to his wood-burning stove

(we all had them then, and Ginsu knives, sump pumps, satellite dishes), then threw them inside, like Shadrach, Meshach, and Abednego,

walked back to the door, slammed it so hard the pictures fell down from the walls.

Still they keep coming, trudging like hoboes, wayward Christian soldiers,

sitting sometimes with a little old lady who offers them cookies and tea.

The worst of them know as they put down their cups that she's not the one

they are witnessing for. The best of them turn, though, mid-Deuteronomy,

as if they know for a minute where Moses was buried,

as if the Red Sea were closing around them,

knowing at that point, knowing full bore,

that she is the Jesus, she is the Jesus,

she can't help be anything else but the Jesus,

so lonely for anything close to a Jesus,

a man in a suit, a knock on the door.

Easter

Twenty minutes before the crowds begin to show,

the regulars, the once-a-years, the ones who come and go,

she appears, freak, car crash, skin graft, so badly burned,

head too big for the world, the woman they let on the Oprah show

to tell us drunk driving victims don't always die like the rest,

that sometimes they fry before the EMT's can get them out.

But today she comes walking, bedecked, grotesque,

past the parking lot of this church in the heart of the Midwest,

where I am sitting, early for once. She looks at me with the eye that is

left, then totters by, past dogwood, spiky grass, the shock of righteous

spring, goes up the church steps one step at a time. I cannot tell you how quiet she is.

Perhaps it has never been quieter here, not since the buffalo have gone.

Now the trains have gone too and the mills have shut down.

Only she is this quiet moving so slowly inside of herself.

She knows the doors of Sacred Heart will be open by now, the great stone

rolled away, the vestibule water waiting sacred, alone,

for her melded, speckled claw-hand to curve inside and touch, in sequence,

her Easter Island head, her harrowed heart, the East and West of her dreams.

Then she will go, Easter done, walk past me again and go home,

having risen so early from the house of the dead, having come

so far, her hand having touched the holiest water,

forgiving us already for all we have done, for how far

we still have to go, for being ourselves, the thing that we are,

for not knowing, for never knowing the thing that we do.

Blind Boy, Fourth of July

Kiwi slices, she tells him. Hundreds of starfish
hanging midair. Dragon castles. Palm trees on fire.

Echoes turn to mushrooms deep in his head.

At the end fusillades, pause, and then boom,
battle horses wandering lost within canyons,
heavy space, broken heart, Hiroshima moon.

She tells him it will be the same way with love,
that love has its history, its Fourth of July,
though she also said once that it lasted forever,
made its own treaties, wore its own sky.

He believes that in time all the stars will fall down,
though she said she would love him till then,
that even in sky death, the whole world gone blind,
she would come to him, stardust in the palms of her hands.
She would tell him they could find errant stars once again,
raise them on kites, float them out across the sky.
He knows it's not true. Then he opens his eyes.

London Letter after the Subway Bombing

Take care, he says at the end, and then, *Take care* again,
my former student letting me know that he is safe and far from harm.
There at St. Mary's Cathedral, along the walls of the nave and anterooms,
the message boards filled with prayers for the ones underground,
slips of colored paper pinned by the faithful, the parishioners,
slim missives, petitions, though the people would not call them that,
handwritten, many-languaged, one in Spanish from a man named Sebastian,
one for Arlene to keep her leg, and one from an anonymous Australian
asking only that his family be kept safe.

Here today the phone books are being delivered on our street, the slow *thunk,*
then *thunk* again, even before the sound of the car can be heard,
like Conrad Aiken's secret snow, as the man in the van tosses one in each driveway,
each in a garish plastic yellow bag. I think how they would look from the air,
little yellow presents, or burning Buddhists at the end of every driveway,
their saffron robes blending neatly with the flames. I think of my neighbor, fifteen
    years ago,
the former Nazi prison guard outed, Wiesenthaled, who up and left that night,
fleeing to Canada to avoid extradition, taking only what he could,
the brightly colored news vans, the action cams showing up in his driveway
the next morning, all of us saying, *He was a quiet man. He waved to the kids,*

and the yellowing newspapers, the mail piling up at his door for weeks,
like waves from some righteous sea having found his shore and run out of breath,
like those who held their papers out for him to see, *Juden, Juden,*
their prayer slips, their yellow stars pinned to their clothing,
the way we pin dollars to statues in parades of the saints,
the way we come out of our houses sometimes, the way we have to come out,

until all of us come, a moving wave, a critical mass, a tipping point,

each with a letter, a petition, an edict, a ribbon, a photograph, a folded flag,

to stick to the emperor to wear as his clothing, his tar and his feathers,

to prick him and sting him, prayer after prayer, *God help us, protect us,*

please don't take my leg, take care of my family, take care, take care, take care.

Dog Dying

The woman I love who no longer loves me

is sitting with her dog who is dying. She holds his head

within her arms and moans his name repeatedly. Flea, she calls him. Flea.

She rocks him slowly back and forth. She will not stop till he is dead.

I leave her message after message on her message machine,

poems and prayers, Updike's "Dog's Death,"

even Rilke's letter about God's joy upon making a dog, the thing seen

at the moment of creation. But she hears only the song of each dying breath,

has grown tired of the sound of my voice. I stop calling.

For her there is only the dog inside the dog as he snuffs at the air,

howls at the moon of his anguish, the blood in his chest rising and falling,

each moment defining if he is or is no longer there.

I pray that he lives. I pray that he dies. One or the other. Soon.

No longer lover. No longer friend. Moon inside the moon.

Jackstaff, Jackstraw (tack and jib)

These the darkling times (that's plain),
these the gathering seas, the bounding *Maine*.

I walk on sunken ships, hip hop, wrap myself in riggings, skin,
swing among the mizzen, Captain Blood. (I'm in like Flynn.)
I John Paul Jones. I Moby Dick. I wail. I win.
I *Lusitania, Arizona* (still got grace, got slick.) Been
blown up, sunk low, the gonfalons a skein
strung out like hopheads, hoptoads in the pouring rain.

I dig this place. I plot my course (my graph, my spade),
shaped up, shipped out. I hover here. I Everglade.
I King Canute. Rock-kneed, I wade,
(behold, betide) and see. But it is always sea.
I cross, I cross. I albatross. I crow's nest constantly.

The land I seek is in your arms, your lighthouse eyes,
a rock-ribbed farm where things take seed, arise,
an island then, a shoal, a spit, a lifeboat filled with loam,
a plug, a stop (we'd make a go of it), a home.
For now (horn blow) I do what Romans do, Horatio. I roam.

Upon Reading that Tatiana Yakovleva, Mayakovsky's Lover, Separated from Him by the Stalin Purges, Had Married and Was Four Months Pregnant when Mayakovsky Killed Himself

Life and I are quits, he said,
and the boat of our love has crashed upon the shore.
And some of the heavy revolver smoke still crept along the ruined floor
like a catamount growling, like an un-trousered cloud,
and poems unfinished, unread, ran away in his blood,
like little stanzas on the colossal page of the sky.
Just then the letter from Paris arrived, with its P.S.
The baby is already moving.

Such movement! Hear me right now, all who have ever loved me
like a gunshot in the night, my *rodnoi*, my kinsmen lost,
all who have ever been hurt by my name, my wounded voice
in the smallest hours, that I have loved you as well,
like a boat in the darkness, that I know now that love comes again
in this world, that I see how clearly the light in the eyes
of the mother out walking with her child is the same light
that moves in the eyes of her daughter holding her hand, looking up,
that it continues, even in the ongoing silence that is our fate,
as sweet as all the faces I have loved, this glow,
this bright flash, this orangery of the heart,
in the baby unborn in your body, the boat upturned on the shore,
the pistol lying bloated in my hand.

Declaration

Every poem is a love poem, she declares.

I smile, say, "Twinkle, Twinkle, Little Star."

She says, How I wonder where you are.

I say, "The Road Not Taken."

She says, That has made all the difference.

I say, "The Midnight Ride of Paul Revere."

She says, The British are coming. The British are coming.

Seriously, I say, he put everything he had on a horse that night,

risked his life for his country. The country of love, she says,

his wife waiting for him in the silvery window, her face like pewter,

the whites of her eyes, the forge of her longing, her smithy heart,

her body, her breathing, warm in his arms, love that had him racing

to reach her again, to hold her so tightly under the moonlight, gleaming,

in his blackened and finely burnished hands, like a poem, don't you think?

ACKNOWLEDGMENTS

Some of these poems originally appeared in the following publications:

Beloit Poetry Journal ("Bootleg," "High Tide," "Look, Look," "Poem to Be Read at 30,000 Feet," "Upon Reading That Abraham Lincoln Spent His Summer Nights as President at a Cottage on the Grounds of the Soldiers' Home on the Outskirts of Washington Rather than at the White House, and that He and Edwin M. Stanton, His Secretary of War, Spent the Better Part of One Evening in 1864 Untangling Two Peacocks that Had Become Ensnared in a Tree," "Watson"); *Crazyhorse* ("Girl with Her Tongue Stuck Out," "Sleep Comes to Mary Todd Lincoln"); *Field* ("Cross-Country," "Girl on the People Mover"); *5 AM* ("Dog Dying"); *Georgia Review* ("Night Rain," "When Dylan Left Hibbing, Minnesota, August, 1959"); *New York Quarterly* ("Killing Mice, December," "Undiscovering America"); *Ploughshares* ("Sorrow"); *Poetry* ("For the Man with the Erection Lasting More than Four Hours"); *Poetry Daily* ("Watson"); *Redactions* ("Overflow"); *Sahara* ("Blind Boy, Fourth of July"); *Slate Magazine* ("At the Optometrist's Office," "Driving Back from Crotched Mountain, Winter Storm, New Year's Eve," "On the Occasion of My Two-Year-Old Granddaughter's First Attempts at an Elvis Impression, I Recall the Difficulties of Her Birth"); *Sun* ("After the Reading, Driving Back to Massachusetts with Jim Beschta, I Think of the Men who Hold the World in Their Hands"); *Willow Springs* ("Upon Seeing a Former Lover Pull Up Next to Me at the Intersection of Metaphysics Lane and Memorial Drive," "Upon Reading a Poem Entitled 'Upon Seeing a Former Lover Pull Up Next to Me at the Intersection of Metaphysics Lane and Memorial Drive,'" "Upon Reading that Tatiana Yakovleva, Mayakovsky's Lover, Separated from Him by the Stalin Purges, Had Married and Was Four Months Pregnant when Mayakovsky Killed Himself," "Witness"); *Worcester Review* ("Teachers," "On Finding My Dead Father at the Worcester Art Museum").

Heaven & Earth Holding Company was designed in Meta Serif with Meta display type and typeset by Kachergis Book Design of Pittsboro, North Carolina.